EROSION AND SINKHOLES

KidHaven
PUBLISHING

TRANSFORMING EARTH'S GEOGRAPHY

Published in 2019 by
KidHaven Publishing, an Imprint of Greenhaven Publishing, LLC
353 3rd Avenue
Suite 255
New York, NY 10010

Designer: Jasmine Pointer
Editor: Holly Duhig

Photo credits: Abbreviations: l–left, r–right, b–bottom, t–top, c–centre, m–middle. Front Cover - Wead. 2 - Sangib Kumar Barman. 4 - Zack Frank. 5t - JoMo333. 5b - Laurens Hoddenbagh. 6 - Vadim Petrakov. 8t - Lee Prince. 8b - neptunestocks. 9 - AG-PHOTOS. 10t - Oleg_Mit. 10m - Jennifer Wan. 10bl - Kennedy Lugo. 10br - Adrian Zenz. 11m - Nico Muller Art. 12t - Caleb Holder. 12b - Everett Historical. 13t - Oleg Znamenskiy. 13b - Nina B. 14t - Niradj. 14b - Jeff Holcombe. 15t - by Paul. 15b - Ekaterina Grivet. 16t - Gustavo Frazao. 16b - Tono Balaguer. 17t - Atlaspix. 17m - Dave Head. 17b - Thomas Barrat. 18t- Galyna Andrushko. 18b - prochasson frederic. 19t - Tono Balaguer. 19b - Yongyut Kumsri. 20 - Andy Cox. 21t - Nicram Sabod. 21b - Evgeny Gorodetsky. 22t - Oscar Espinosa. 22b - Rich Lindie. 23l - Dennis van de Water. 23r - shell300. 24t - FiledIMAGE. 24bl - Stanislav Fosenbauer. 25t - adkana. 25b - Peter Zurek. 26t - Wolfgang Zwanzger. 26b - Dario Lo Presti. 27t - Stepo_1107. 27b - SL Chen. 28t - Valdis Skudre. 28b - John_Walker. 29 - Wollertz. 30t - Vietnam Stock Images. 30br - Ky Doan. Images are courtesy of Shutterstock.com. With thanks to Getty Images, Thinkstock Photo and iStockphoto.

Cataloging-in-Publication Data

Names: Brundle, Joanna.
Title: Erosion and sinkholes / Joanna Brundle.
Description: New York : KidHaven Publishing, 2019. | Series: Transforming Earth's geography | Includes glossary and index.
Identifiers: ISBN 9781534528918 (pbk.) | ISBN 9781534528932 (library bound) | ISBN 9781534528925 (6 pack) | ISBN 9781534528949 (ebook)
Subjects: LCSH: Erosion–Juvenile literature. | Sinkholes–Juvenile literature.
Classification: LCC QE571.B78 2019 | DDC 551.3'02–dc2

Printed in the United States of America

CPSIA compliance information: Batch #BW19KL: For further information contact Greenhaven Publishing LLC, New York, New York at 1-844-317-7404.

Please visit our website, www.greenhavenpublishing.com. For a free color catalog of all our high-quality books, call toll free 1-844-317-7404 or fax 1-844-317-7405.

EROSION AND SINKHOLES

CONTENTS

Page 4	What Is Erosion?
Page 6	River Erosion
Page 8	Rainfall Erosion
Page 10	Coastal Erosion
Page 12	Wind Erosion
Page 14	Glacial Erosion
Page 16	How Do Humans Affect Erosion?
Page 18	The Grand Canyon, USA
Page 20	The Moeraki Boulders, New Zealand
Page 22	Tsingy de Bemaraha, Madagascar
Page 24	Uluru
Page 26	What Are Sinkholes?
Page 28	Blue Holes
Page 30	Hang Son Doong, Vietnam
Page 31	Glossary
Page 32	Index

Words that look like **this** can be found in the glossary on page 31.

WHAT IS EROSION?

If you think about some of the features of Earth's surface, like mountains and coastlines, they seem solid and permanent don't they? In fact, Earth's surface is constantly changing and being reshaped by the forces of water, wind, and ice. Two processes, weathering and erosion, work together to make this happen.

WEATHERING AND EROSION — WHAT'S THE DIFFERENCE?

Weathering is the natural process that breaks rocks down over time. Erosion is the moving of these smaller pieces of weathered rock, as well as dissolved soil or material, from one place on Earth's surface to another.

Rock Formations in Mammoth Caves, Kentucky, USA

If a substance has dissolved, it means that it has been absorbed into a liquid, to form a solution.

These caves, which are some of the largest in the world, were formed by underground erosion caused by rainwater.

Although some rocks are harder than others, no rock is strong enough to withstand the forces of weathering and erosion.

Weathering must happen before erosion can take place.

TYPES OF WEATHERING

Weathering happens in different ways. **Biological** weathering can be caused by plants and animals. Tree roots, for example, may grow into cracks in rocks, eventually breaking pieces away. Physical weathering may be caused by rainwater seeping into cracks. As it freezes, water expands. This gradually breaks up rock as the water thaws and refreezes. This is called freeze-thaw weathering.

HOW LONG DOES EROSION TAKE?

Erosion can take minutes or millions of years. **Flash floods** can move soil, rocks, and debris rapidly. But it takes thousands of years for slow-moving masses of ice, called glaciers, to carve out mountain valleys.

Basalt cliffs in Iceland

Physical weathering has broken off pieces of these cliffs. Erosion has happened when the pieces have fallen to the base.

This deep valley was carved out by a glacier during the last ice age, when the climate changed and the planet was much colder.

Fjord in Norway

RIVER EROSION

A river flows from high to low ground, eventually reaching the sea. On this journey, a river causes erosion as it carries soil and rock particles further downstream. The material carried by the river may be pushed and rolled along the riverbed by the force of the moving water. It may also be carried along in the flow, either dissolved or **suspended** in the water. As it moves closer to the sea, a river loses its energy and begins to drop the material it has been carrying. This is called deposition.

Aerial View of the Okavango Delta, Botswana, Africa

New landforms, such as a delta, may gradually form as a river drops its eroded material.

TYPES OF RIVER EROSION

01 **ABRASION**
The riverbed and banks are gradually worn away by rocks and debris carried along by the water.

ATTRITION
Rocks carried by the river crash into one another to form smaller, smoother rocks.
02

03 **SOLUTION**
As it travels, the river picks up particles that dissolve into it.

HYDRAULIC ACTION
A river can trap air in cracks and crevices along its banks. This gradually weakens and wears away parts of the bank, which are carried away by the water.
04

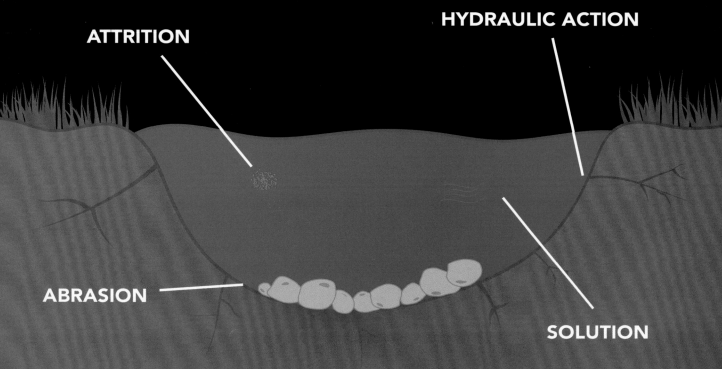

HYDRAULIC ACTION

ATTRITION

ABRASION

SOLUTION

RAINFALL EROSION

Rainfall can lead to soil erosion. The heaviness of the rain, the slope of the land, and the amount of vegetation – plant material including trees, bushes, and grasses – covering the land all affect soil erosion. On a slope, water runs off easily, taking soil with it. Vegetation cover helps to hold soil together and helps water to drain away before erosion can take place.

Rainwater running off down the slope where these trees are growing has gradually eroded the soil, exposing the roots.

ACID RAIN

A gas in the air called carbon dioxide can dissolve in rainwater to form a weak acid. Acids dissolve things, so when rainwater is acidic, it can dissolve rocks. This is called chemical weathering and happens when the minerals in rocks react with the acidic rainwater. As the water runs away, erosion of the rock occurs.

UNDERGROUND EROSION

Stalactites

Stalagmites

Limestone caves often have interesting features such as stalactites and stalagmites.

Underground caves are formed when rainwater seeps into limestone and other porous rocks such as dolomite, gypsum, and marble. Limestone is a sedimentary rock, which means it has been laid down in layers. It has horizontal blocks called bedding planes and vertical cracks called joints.

As the water percolates through, it gradually dissolves the rock, making the gaps in the rock larger and larger until, eventually, caves are formed. Underground streams carry away the dissolved material. They may reappear as springs at the base of limestone structures.

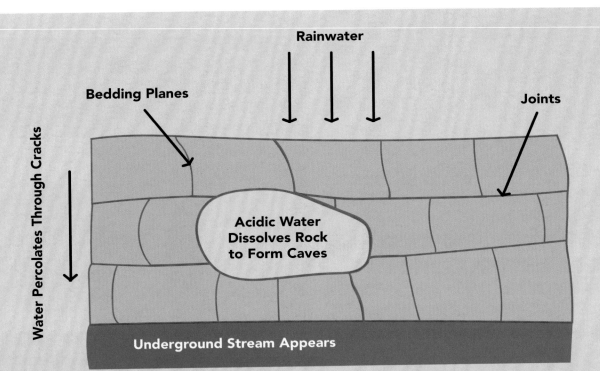

Rainwater

Bedding Planes

Joints

Water Percolates Through Cracks

Acidic Water Dissolves Rock to Form Caves

Underground Stream Appears

COASTAL EROSION

Coastal erosion is the gradual wearing away, breaking up, and movement of rock along the coastline. Sea caves form when waves force their way into cracks in a cliff face. Sections of weaker rock in the cliff face are gradually worn away by sand and other material in the water to form caves.

Headlands are formed on coasts with bands of soft and hard rocks. The softer rocks, like clay, are eroded by the sea, leaving harder rocks, like chalk, sticking out into the sea.

Undercut cliffs are caused by pounding waves.

A Headland in California, USA

Durdle Door in Dorset, England, is an example of a natural limestone arch.

Stacks continue to be eroded by the waves and eventually collapse into the sea, leaving a stump.

ARCHES AND STACKS

If two caves form on either side of a headland, further erosion may eventually join them together. This forms an arch that you can walk or swim through.

Stacks are formed when further erosion wears away the roof of an arch, causing it to fall into the sea.

Coastal Stacks in Wales

10

HOW ARE BEACHES FORMED?

As the sea erodes cliffs, rocks fall into the sea by the force of **gravity**. These large, sharp-edged rocks are tossed around by the sea and are gradually worn away into smoother, rounded rocks. Further erosion produces smaller and smaller pebbles. These pebbles are eventually ground down into shingle and tiny grains of sand.

LONGSHORE DRIFT

Longshore drift is a natural process in which the sea carries sand, pebbles, and sediment sideways along the coast. Material that has been removed from the coastline in one place is transported by longshore drift and forms new land when it is deposited further along the coast.

You can see the zigzag pattern for yourself if you throw an inflatable ball into the sea and watch where it moves in the waves.

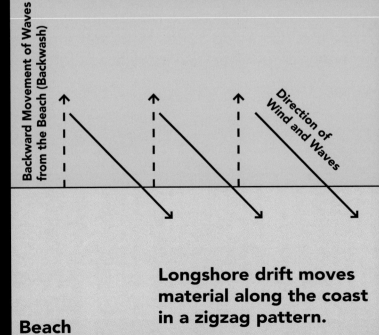

Backward Movement of Waves from the Beach (Backwash)

Direction of Wind and Waves

Beach

Longshore drift moves material along the coast in a zigzag pattern.

WIND EROSION

Dust Storm

Wind can also cause soil erosion. This often happens in flat, bare areas with loose, dry soils. Light winds roll soil particles along the surface. This is called surface creep. Strong winds lift large volumes of soil into the air and create dust storms.

SOIL EROSION IN THE GREAT PLAINS

In the 1930s, the Great Plains of the United States suffered high temperatures and little rain. The soil turned to dust. High winds eroded the dry soil, causing dust storms and damaging crops. Trees and shrubs that had once held the soil together had been removed to give more space for farming.

Eroded soil was carried in the wind and buried homes and farm buildings.

VENTIFACTS AND HOODOOS

Over thousands of years, winds that blow sand and small rock particles can wear away rocks. In the deserts of North Africa stand strange rock formations that have been eroded by sand particles carried in the wind. When the area became a desert around 7,000 years ago, wind erosion began to form the unusual shapes that are visible today. Wind erosion attacks only the base of the structures because the sand particles are too heavy to be lifted very high into the air. This produces mushroom-shaped formations.

Limestone rock formation in the White Desert, Egypt

Stones that have been eroded by sand being carried in the wind are known as ventifacts. They are almost always found in desert areas.

Goblin Valley, Utah, USA

Wind erosion of sandstone rock created these rock formations, known as hoodoos.

GLACIAL EROSION

Glaciers form when layers of snow are compressed to form ice. Eventually, the weight of the ice and the force of gravity cause the glacier to begin moving slowly downhill. As a glacier moves, it erodes the landscape, carving out new landforms. This is why glaciers are sometimes called "nature's bulldozers."

Fox Glacier

Although most common in Antarctica and the Arctic, glaciers are found in the mountains of every continent except Australia.

The world's fastest-moving glacier, the Jakobshavn Isbrae in Greenland, covers around 130 feet (40 m) a day. Fox Glacier in New Zealand travels less than 2 feet (0.5 m) a day.

PLUCKING AND ABRASION

Meltwater at the base of a glacier refreezes around lumps of cracked, broken rock. As the glacier moves downhill, this rock is pulled away from the mountainside. This is called plucking. As the glacier continues its journey, rock frozen to the bottom of the glacier grinds away the rock below, rather like sandpaper. This is called abrasion.

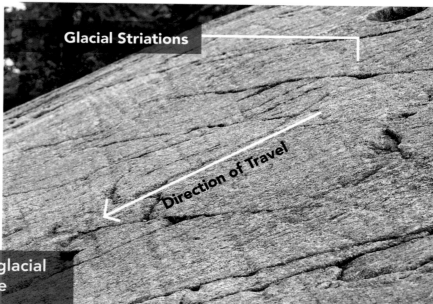

Glacial Striations

Direction of Travel

Long scratches in rock, known as glacial striations, show that a glacier once passed over the area.

GLACIAL FEATURES

During the last ice age, glaciers covered parts of the world that are now much warmer. Although the ice age glaciers have melted, the landforms that they carved out are still visible. Glaciers that moved through river valleys gouged out U-shaped valleys with steep sides and wide, flat bases.

U-Shaped Glacial Valley

Arêtes are thin crests of rock left after two glaciers have worn away the rock on either side. When glaciers erode three or more arêtes, a landform known as a horn is formed. Horns are sharp-edged mountain peaks.

The Matterhorn in Switzerland is a well-known example of a horn.

Arête

HOW DO HUMANS AFFECT EROSION?

Some human activities speed up erosion. Trees and plants provide ground cover and protection from the wind, while their roots hold soil together. If this vegetation is removed to provide land for farms, ranches, buildings, and roads, it can lead to soil erosion by wind and rainfall.

Deforestation, which is the cutting down or burning of forests, has the same effect. The wash from boats and ferries on rivers and lakes can cause erosion of the riverbanks. Humans can reduce the effects of erosion by planting ground cover, trees, and hedges and by reducing deforestation.

Deforestation removes the protection from soil erosion that the thick canopy and root systems of rainforests provide.

The activities of small animals and insects may break up soil, making it easier for wind and rainwater to erode.

Speed limits on waterways can help to reduce the erosion of the banks caused by wash from boats.

COASTAL DEFENSES

Man-made defenses, such as seawalls and boulder barriers, absorb some of the energy of the waves hitting the coastline. This helps to protect the base of cliffs, land, and buildings from erosion, as well as helping to prevent flooding.

Seawall

Boulder Barrier

Beaches are a natural protection against the erosion of cliffs, but they themselves can be eroded by the sea. Groynes are wooden structures built along a beach and out into the sea. They allow beaches to build up between them, and help to stop sand and other material being removed by longshore drift.

Groynes

Sand that has been removed by erosion and longshore drift may be replaced by humans. This is called beach management.

THE GRAND CANYON, USA

Canyons are deep, narrow valleys between steep cliffs. They are formed by weathering and erosion from a river, which slowly cuts its way down through the surrounding rock. The Grand Canyon in northern Arizona is one of the largest canyons in the world.

The canyon is 277 miles (446 km) long, up to 18 miles (29 km) wide and, at its maximum depth, 6,093 feet (1,857 m) deep!

The Grand Canyon is so vast that it can be clearly seen from space.

HOW WAS THE GRAND CANYON FORMED?

Earth's crust is constantly moving, creating huge forces. Millions of years ago, these forces pushed the rocks that form the Colorado Plateau upwards. In turn, this forced the Colorado River to carve its way back down through the rocks, creating the canyon.

The Colorado Plateau is a huge, flat, raised landform, located where the states of Utah, Arizona, Colorado, and New Mexico meet.

Utah

Colorado

Colorado Plateau

Grand Canyon

Arizona

New Mexico

WEATHERING AND EROSION

The Grand Canyon is still being widened and made deeper by weathering and erosion. Its extreme temperatures cause freeze-thaw weathering in winter. Scorching summer temperatures of over 104°F (40°C) in places cause the rocks to expand and contract. This weathering weakens the rocks, which split and break off, gradually widening the canyon. The Colorado River carries around 500,000 tons of sand and silt every day. This acts like liquid sandpaper, eroding the canyon, making it wider and deeper.

The different rock layers – or strata – reveal a cross section of Earth's crust going back nearly two billion years.

Antelope Canyon, Arizona

The sweeping shapes of Antelope Canyon, close to the Grand Canyon, were eroded over millions of years by wind, rain, and flash floods.

THE MORAKI BOULDERS, NEW ZEALAND

Close to the New Zealand fishing village of Moeraki is Koekohe Beach.
On the beach is a startling sight – a collection of huge, rounded boulders.

There are over 50 boulders along Koekohe Beach, found both in clusters and alone.

The largest boulders took over four million years to reach their current size.

The boulders formed in a deposit of mud and sediment on the seabed. Some of the sediment was hardened by the action of other minerals. This process is called concretion. The hardened rock was buried in cliffs made of a rock called mudstone. Concretion made the boulders harder than the surrounding mudstone. Coastal erosion of the cliffs then gradually removed the softer mudstone, exposing the boulders buried inside.

South Island, New Zealand

Oamaru

Moeraki ··········<· Moeraki Boulders

The boulders began to form around 56 million years ago.

The largest boulders weigh around 7 tons and are nearly 7 feet (2 m) in diameter. The hard outer surfaces of the boulders are lined with cracks called septaria. These cracks spread out from the partly hollow, softer centers of the boulders. The cracks are filled with minerals including quartz and calcite, which give the boulders their unusual appearance.

Cracks on the surface of the boulders make them look like soccer balls or turtle eggs.

This cracked boulder clearly shows the hollow center.

Ancient drawings of the beach suggest that originally, there were many more boulders than are visible today. Some smaller boulders may have been removed by visitors as souvenirs.

Since 1971, Koekohe Beach has been a protected scientific site.

TSINGY DE BEMARAHA, MADAGASCAR

Tsingy de Bemaraha is a national park and nature reserve near the western coast of Madagascar. It covers about 587 square miles (1,520 sq km), around half of which is covered in tall, spiky rock formations. These are made of limestone and look somewhat like a forest of stone. Trees and shrubs grow between the pinnacles, which can reach up to 330 feet (100 m) in height. The harsh conditions are home to iguanas, frogs, lemurs, chameleons, over 100 bird species, and around 650 plant species.

An unexplored network of limestone caves lies beneath Tsingy de Bemaraha.

Tsingy de Bemaraha is an appropriate name – in the local Malagasy language, "tsingy" means "where one cannot walk barefoot" or "to tiptoe."

Decken's sifaka lemur is well adapted to its environment, jumping nimbly between the rocks and trees.

Tsingy de Bemaraha

Madagascar

HOW WAS TSINGY DE BEMARAHA FORMED?

Around 200 million years ago, a thick limestone bed formed at the bottom of a **Jurassic lagoon**. Movements in the Earth's crust lifted the limestone bed upwards. During the ice ages, sea levels dropped. The limestone bed was now no longer underwater and was gradually eroded by heavy rains. Rivers and streams carved out caves and tunnels as the limestone dissolved. Eventually, the roofs of the caves and tunnels collapsed. This created narrow canyons and gorges, edged by pinnacles of rock.

Narrow Canyon

Walkways and rope bridges allow visitors with a head for heights to take a closer look.

Some of the canyons are so narrow that it would be difficult for a human to pass through.

Tsingy de Bemaraha continues to be eroded by wind and heavy rainfall – up to 59 inches (150 cm) a year.

ULURU

Uluru is made of gray sandstone, but iron compounds in the rock form red iron oxide (rust) at the surface, giving the rock a red appearance at sunrise and sunset.

Uluru

For the native Aboriginal people, Uluru is a sacred place.

Uluru, also known as Ayers Rock, lies in the center of Australia, in the southwest corner of the Northern Territory. It's an **inselberg**, or island mountain, and is one of Australia's most famous landmarks.

The **circumference** of Uluru is 5.8 miles (9.4 km) and it is 1,150 feet (350 m) tall. The Aboriginal people originally inhabited the area about 10,000 years ago, and caves within Uluru are decorated with their art.

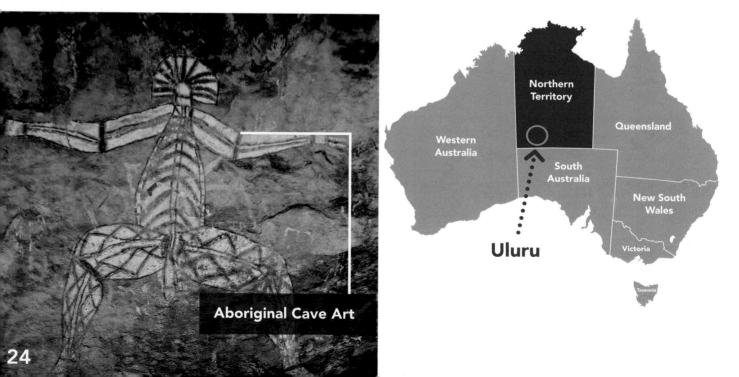

Aboriginal Cave Art

Western Australia

Northern Territory

Queensland

South Australia

New South Wales

Victoria

Tasmania

Uluru

The rock that forms Uluru was originally at the bottom of a large ocean. Huge forces resulting from movements in Earth's crust tilted the rock layers. This exposed the layered sandstone bed that is visible today. The hard sandstone rock was left behind after softer surrounding rock had been eroded away. Uluru has gradually been eroded into rounded forms by desert storms. Ridges and valleys on the surface and caves beneath have been eroded by rainwater. No vegetation grows on Uluru, leaving it exposed to erosion by wind and rain.

These hikers give an idea of the size of Uluru.

Erosion has created caves and strange formations in Uluru.

Uluru is believed to have formed around 600 million years ago, long before dinosaurs roamed Earth.

WHAT ARE SINKHOLES?

Sinkholes are holes in the ground caused by the collapse of the ground surface. They are common in areas where the bedrock is limestone or other rock, such as gypsum, that can be dissolved by water. This type of area is called karst landscape. As rainwater seeps through cracks, the rock is gradually weathered and eroded underground, forming a hollow area. Eventually, the surface rock and soil can no longer be supported and the surface suddenly collapses inward, forming a sinkhole. This is called a cover-collapse sinkhole.

Bimmah sinkhole, Oman

Cover-subsidence sinkholes form slowly where sand filters down into rock beneath and the exposed surface rock is gradually eroded, forming a dip.

Sinkholes often fill with water and may connect to underground tunnels, rivers and caves.

Sinkholes are also called shakeholes, swallets, swallow holes, cenotes, and dolines.

Can you see rocky outcrops of the limestone that form the bedrock of this karst landscape?

This is the Pulo of Altamura, a large sinkhole in southern Italy.

Sinkholes can be less than a few feet in width or large enough to swallow up cars and buildings. Cover-collapse sinkholes appear to form very suddenly, but the underground erosion that causes them may have developed over thousands of years.

The Crveno Jezero – or "Red Lake" – sinkhole, in Croatia, is named after the reddish-brown color of the cliffs.

The actions of humans may also cause sinkholes to appear. Disused mine shafts and tunnels can collapse underground. Badly maintained sewers and underground pipes can cause water to leak out and erode the rock beneath the surface.

Buildings, roads, and paved areas can stop rainwater from draining away, causing runoff to collect in a particular area. This may eventually erode the ground, causing a sinkhole.

This sinkhole in Kuala Lumpur, Malaysia, opened up after very heavy rains and swallowed up traffic lights and power lines.

Space scientists have found evidence of sinkholes on Mars.

BLUE HOLES

Blue holes are underwater sinkholes. They were formed during previous ice ages when sea levels were hundreds of feet lower than they are today. Areas that are underwater today were dry land at that time. Meltwater from melting snow and ice, percolating through areas of limestone, weathered and eroded the rock. This formed caves. Further erosion eventually caused the caves to collapse, forming sinkholes. At the end of the ice ages, sea levels rose, flooding the sinkholes. This formed deep round holes in the ocean floor, known as blue holes.

In July 2016, scientists discovered the world's deepest underwater sinkhole in the South China Sea. The Dragon Hole is about 985 feet (300 m) deep, similar to the height of the Shard.

This image of the Shard in London, UK, gives an idea of the great depth of the Dragon Hole.

The 425-foot-deep Blue Hole in the Red Sea off the coast of Egypt is popular with scuba divers.

28

THE GREAT BLUE HOLE

The Great Blue Hole lies near the center of Lighthouse Reef off the coast of Belize. It is a perfectly round hole in the middle of an atoll. More than 15,000 years ago, erosion caused the roof of a limestone cave to collapse, creating a huge sinkhole more than 400 feet (120 m) deep. Rising sea levels at the end of the ice ages then flooded the sinkhole. Stalactites and stalagmites can still be seen in the natural underwater passageways and caves at the bottom of the hole.

An aerial view of the Great Blue Hole

The turquoise water of the shallow coral reef highlights the deep blue water of the hole.

Jacques Cousteau, a famous French marine biologist, was the first to explore the Great Blue Hole in 1972.

HANG SON DOONG, VIETNAM

Hang Son Doong in Phong Nha-Ke Bang National Park, Vietnam, is the largest cave in the world. It is 650 feet (200 m) high in places, 500 feet (150 m) wide, and around 3 miles (5 km) long. Two huge sinkholes formed when parts of the roof of the cave collapsed. These sinkholes allow light to enter and plants to grow. Hang Son Doong is so vast that it has its own river, jungle, and climate with underground clouds.

Hang Son Doong means "cave of the mountain river."

Entrance to Hang Son Doong

The cave was formed by the Rao Thuong river. It gradually eroded the limestone bedrock, forming the tunnel-like cave beneath the Annamite Mountains.

China

Vietnam

Laos

Hang Son Doong

Thailand

Cambodia

Thien Duong, or Paradise Cave, is part of the same cave system and is full of beautiful rock formations.

GLOSSARY

atoll	a ring-shaped coral island
bedrock	the lower layer of Earth's crust, made of solid rock
biological	relating to a living organism, such as a plant or animal
carbon dioxide	a natural, colorless gas found in the air
circumference	the distance around something
cross section	a view into the inside of something made by cutting through it
delta	a triangular area at the mouth of a river where eroded material is deposited, forming swampy islands
Earth's crust	the outermost layer of Earth, made up of different types of rock
flash floods	sudden, local, short-lived floods caused by heavy rain or by the blockage of a river
gravity	the force that pulls everything down towards the center of Earth
inselberg	a hill or small mountain that rises up on its own from a surrounding flat area that has been eroded away
Jurassic	referring to a period of time from 208 to 146 million years ago
lagoon	a shallow lake or pool, usually connected to the sea but protected from it by a sandbar or coral reef
marine biologist	a scientist who studies organisms that live in salt water
meltwater	water that has come from melting snow or ice, particularly a glacier
minerals	natural, sometimes valuable substances found in Earth's crust
percolates	gradually passes through a porous substance
porous	able to absorb liquids or allow them to pass through
sediment	small pieces of rock, minerals, and animal and plant remains, which are carried by erosion from one place to another
suspended	carried between the top and bottom layers of a material such as water or air

INDEX

A

abrasion 7, 14

arches 10

arêtes 15

attrition 7

B

beach management 17

beaches 11,17, 20–21

blue holes 28–29

C

canyons 18–19, 23

caves 4, 9–10, 22–26, 28–30

cliffs 5, 8, 10–11, 17–18, 20, 27

coastal defenses 17

coasts 4, 10–11, 17, 20, 22, 28–29

concretion 20

D

deforestation 16

deposition 6

E

erosion

. coastal 10–11, 20

. glacial 14–15

. rainfall 8–9

. river 6–7

. soil 8, 12, 16

. underground 4, 9, 27

. wind 12–13

F

fjords 5

flash floods 5, 19

G

glaciers 5, 14–15

groynes 17

H

headlands 10

horns 15

L

limestone 9–10, 13, 22–23,26, 28–30

M

mountains 4–5, 14–15, 24

R

rainfall 8–9, 16, 23

rivers 6–7, 15–16, 18–19, 23, 26, 30

S

stacks 10

stalactites 9, 29

stalagmites 9, 29

striations 14

stumps 10

V

valleys 5, 13, 15, 18, 25

vegetation 8, 16, 25

W

weathering

. biological 5

. chemical 8

. freeze-thaw 5, 19

. physical 5

DIY FOR BOYS

ROUGHING IT

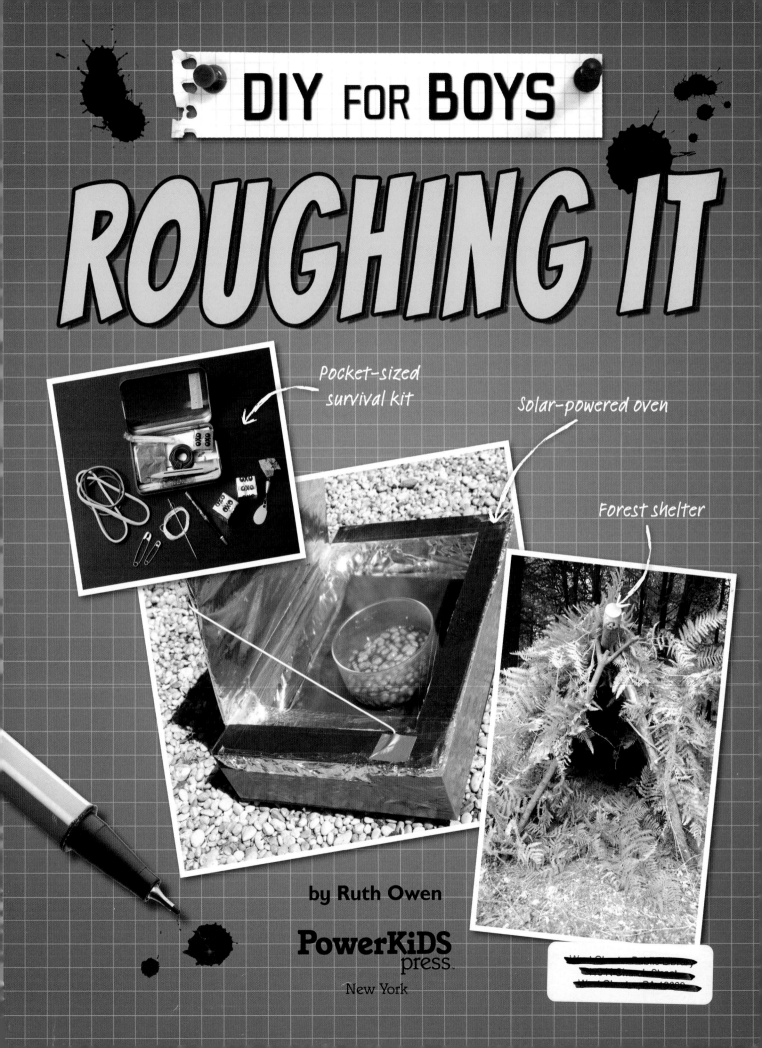

Pocket-sized survival kit

Solar-powered oven

Forest shelter

by Ruth Owen

PowerKiDS press™

New York

Published in 2014 by The Rosen Publishing Group, Inc.
29 East 21st Street, New York, NY 10010

Produced for Rosen by Ruby Tuesday Books Ltd
Editor for Ruby Tuesday Books Ltd: Mark J. Sachner
US Editor: Joshua Shadowens
Designers: Tammy West and Emma Randall

With special thanks to Steve Owen for his help in developing and making
the projects in this book.

Photo Credits:
Cover, 1, 5, 6—7, 8—9, 10—11, 13, 21, 22, 24—25, 26—27, 28—29 © Ruby Tuesday
Books and John Such; cover, 1, 14, 16—17 © Emily Heath; 1, 4—5, 12—13, 15, 16—17,
18—19, 20—21, 22—23, 24, 27 © Shutterstock.

Library of Congress Cataloging-in-Publication Data

Owen, Ruth.
 Roughing it / Ruth Owen.
    pages cm. — (DIY for boys)
 Includes index.
 ISBN 978-1-4777-6278-3 (library binding) — ISBN 978-1-4777-6279-0 (pbk.) —
 ISBN 978-1-4777-6280-6 (6-pack)
 1. Wilderness survival—Juvenile literature. I. Title.
 GV200.5.O95 2014
 613.6'9—dc23
                          2013035234

Manufactured in the United States of America

CPSIA Compliance Information: Batch #W14PK8 For Further Information contact: Rosen Publishing, New York, New York at 1-800-237-9932

CONTENTS

Going Wild! 4

Pocket-Sized Survival Kit 6

A DIY Compass 12

Build a Forest Shelter 14

Building a Campfire 18

Build a Solar-Powered Oven 24

Make a Pot-in-a-Pot Cooler 28

Glossary 30

Websites 31

Read More, Index 32

WARNING!

Neither the author nor the publisher shall be liable for any bodily harm or damage to property that may happen as a result of carrying out the projects in this book.

In your everyday life, water comes from a tap, a hot snack comes from the microwave, and your house or apartment keeps you warm and dry. If you're spending time outdoors camping or hiking, however, you can't always rely on these comforts. That's where this book comes in!

If you're going to be roughing it in forests or other wild places, this book shows you how to make a **survival kit**, light a fire without matches, and even build a shelter from branches and leaves!

If hanging out with friends in your backyard is more your thing, there are fun projects that show you how to turn flowerpots into a cooler to keep your drinks chilled, and how to make an oven powered by the Sun.

survival
kit

5

Any trip into a **wilderness** area should be carefully planned. When you're roughing it, however, unexpected things can happen. For example, you might get lost in a forest and not be able to find your way back to your camp.

WARNING:
Only use a glue gun or work with a craft knife and matches if an adult is there to help you.

Therefore, it's helpful to always carry a survival kit in your pocket. You can never **anticipate** what might go wrong, so pack your kit with lots of useful everyday items.

On the next few pages, you will find suggestions for putting together a survival kit. Find ways to **utilize** every tiny bit of space inside the kit and include as many items as possible.

YOU WILL NEED:

- A small tin or plastic container
- Duct tape
- Scissors
- A glue gun
- A pencil sharpener
- Survival items for the kit as required

STEP 1:

Find a pocket-sized plastic container or tin. The type of tin that holds mints works well. Then begin putting together the components of your survival kit.

STEP 2:

To make a small, but simple knife, take a craft knife blade and wrap one edge with duct tape. The duct tape makes a safe edge for holding.

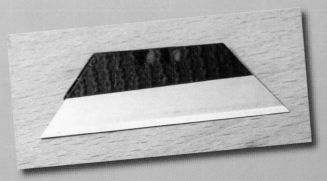

STEP 3:

For safety, but also to utilize every tiny bit of space inside the kit, tape the knife inside the box or tin's lid using duct tape.

STEP 4:

If you want to carry matches, glue the striker from a matchbook inside the lid of the box or tin. Tightly wrap some matches in plastic wrap to keep them dry.

Match striker

STEP 5:

A pencil could be useful, so snap a pencil into a short length that will fit inside your kit. Sharpen both ends.

Seal one end of a straw with hot glue.

Liquid

Seal the other end with glue.

STEP 6:

To make mini containers for holding antiseptic for cuts, hand cleanser, or other liquids, cut a drinking straw into short lengths. Place a blob of hot glue at one end of a straw, then squeeze the end of the straw so it seals up. Fill the straw with liquid, then seal the other end using hot glue.

STEP 7:

If you will be near water, put together a basic selection of equipment for catching fish.

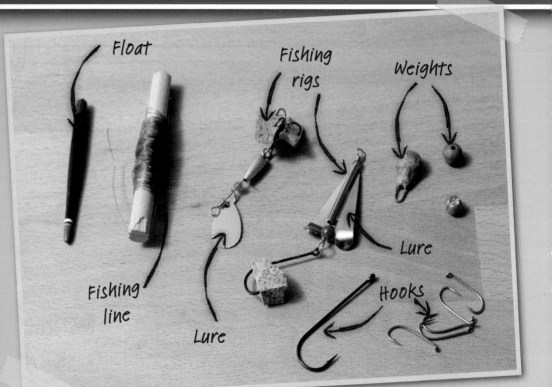

Float

Fishing rigs

Weights

Fishing line

Lure

Lure

Hooks

STEP 8:

A large sheet of aluminum foil can be used for collecting water or for wrapping around food so it can be cooked on an open fire.

Fold up the foil as small as you can.

STEP 9:

Try to think of items that might be useful and fit as many as possible into your survival kit.

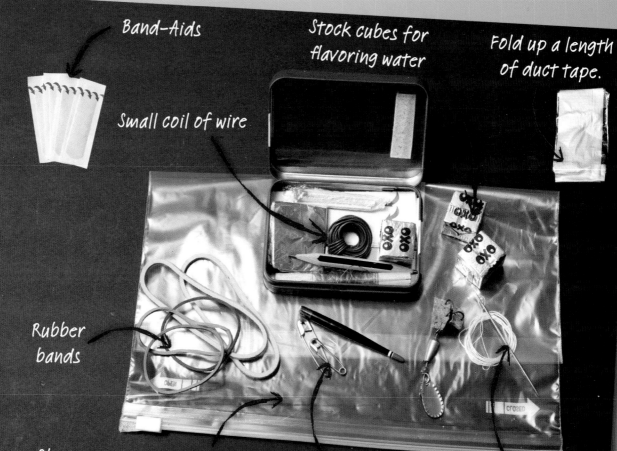

Band-Aids

Stock cubes for flavoring water

Fold up a length of duct tape.

Small coil of wire

Rubber bands

Plastic sandwich baggie

Safety pins

Needle and thread

STEP 10:

To save space inside the kit and to keep it secure, wrap the rubber bands around the outside of the box or tin.

A DIY COMPASS

A **compass** is an essential piece of equipment when you're hiking or spending time in the wilderness.

No matter which direction you turn, the needle in a compass will always point north. This is because the needle is pulled to the north by the natural magnetism of the Earth. A compass allows you to figure out if you are walking to the north, east, south, or west. This will help you stay on a straight path, and not walk around in circles, if you are in an environment, such as a forest, where everything looks the same in all directions.

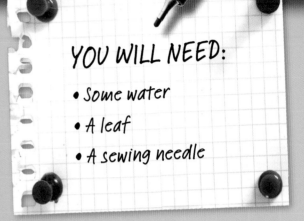

YOU WILL NEED:
- Some water
- A leaf
- A sewing needle

You can add a tiny compass to your survival kit, or make your own using just some water, a leaf, and the sewing needle from your survival kit.

A compass

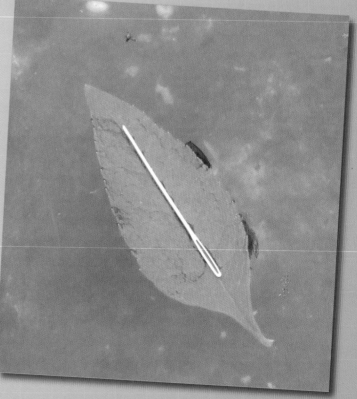

STEP 1:

Find a small flat leaf and some water, such as a puddle.

STEP 2:

Float the leaf on the puddle.

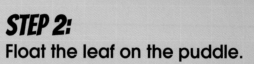

STEP 3:

Gently place the needle onto the leaf.

Now that the needle is floating on water it can move freely. Like the needle in a compass, the Earth's magnetism will pull the point of the needle toward north. You need to use a leaf, like a raft, beneath the needle to stop the needle from sinking.

STEP 4:

To be sure your leaf and needle compass is working, you can test it two or three times by gently moving the leaf with your finger so the needle is pointing in a different direction. Each time, the needle and leaf will slowly turn and come to a stop with the needle pointing north.

BUILD A FOREST SHELTER

If you're spending time in a wilderness environment, you'll probably carry a tent with you. It's important, however, to know how to build a shelter if no tent is available. A well-built shelter can protect you from sun, rain, wind, and snow.

If you're in a forest, you can build a **debris** hut in just one or two hours. This type of shelter is made from debris, or materials, such as branches, leaves, tree bark, and **moss**. If you're carrying a jackknife, it will be very useful for cutting branches. It's possible, however, to make this shelter without using any tools at all.

A debris hut

STEP 1:

Begin by finding a long, thick, straight branch that will be the hut's ridgepole. When making your hut, try to find material that has fallen onto the forest floor. If you need to cut or break branches off trees, only take what you will use.

YOU WILL NEED:

- A long, thick, straight branch
- Other assorted branches
- A jackknife (if available)
- Wire, rubber bands, or other binding material from a survival kit
- Debris such as leafy branches, fern leaves, tree bark, and moss

STEP 2:

To make the hut's frame, create a tripod using the ridgepole and two shorter branches.

You can bind the three branches together using wire or the rubber bands from your survival kit.

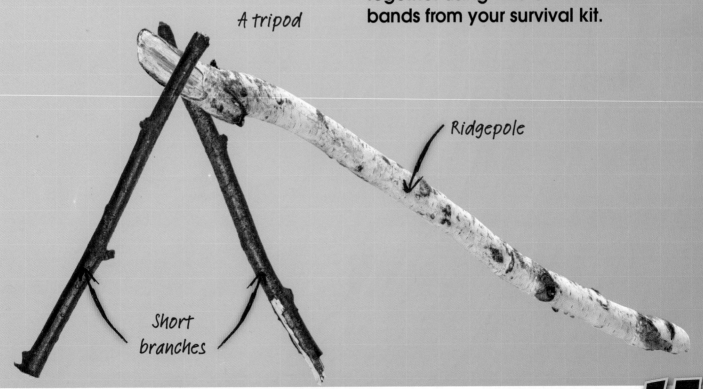

A tripod

Ridgepole

Short branches

STEP 3:
Alternatively, find a tree stump and lean the ridgepole against the stump.

Ridgepole

Tree stump

STEP 4:
Collect sticks in different lengths.

STEP 5:
Prop the sticks along both sides of the ridgepole to create ribbing. The hut's frame is now complete.

Ridgepole

Sticks of different lengths

STEP 6:

Next, gather material, or debris, to cover the frame. Leafy branches, pine tree branches, large fern leaves, bark, and moss all work well.

Pine tree branch

Bark

Fern leaf

Moss

STEP 7:

Cover the frame with a thick layer of debris. In a cold weather survival situation, you would need to cover the hut in debris that's 3 feet (1 m) deep!

STEP 8:

Cover the ground inside the hut with leaves and other soft debris.

BUILDING A CAMPFIRE

In a survival situation, a campfire will keep you warm and give you comfort. Of course you can light a fire with matches, but if you don't have matches, here's a way to start a fire using the Sun, a plastic water bottle, and some paper.

Knowing how to build and start a fire is an important survival skill. You should never try to light a fire without an adult being present, however. Also, did you know that in the United States, 9 out of 10 **wildfires** are started by people being careless? So when you're roughing it, follow the fire safety rules on these pages. Enjoy using your outdoor skills, but be responsible, protect the wild places you visit, and stay safe.

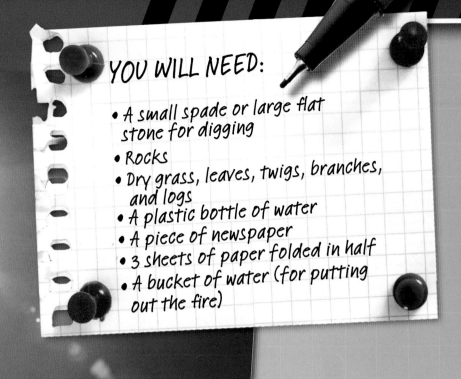

YOU WILL NEED:

- A small spade or large flat stone for digging
- Rocks
- Dry grass, leaves, twigs, branches, and logs
- A plastic bottle of water
- A piece of newspaper
- 3 sheets of paper folded in half
- A bucket of water (for putting out the fire)

STEP 1:

You will need the Sun to be shining in order to light your fire. The Sun's light must also be able to easily reach the place where you are working.

STEP 2:

Choose a spot to build your fire where there are no trees, plants, or dry grasses within 10 feet (3 m) of the fire.

STEP 3:

Clear any debris that might catch fire from a spark, such as dry leaves or twigs, from the 10-foot (3-m) radius of the fire. Save these materials to use as tinder to start the fire.

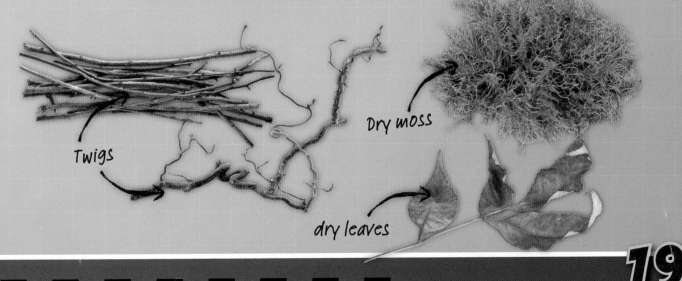

Twigs

Dry moss

dry leaves

STEP 4:

Dig or scrape a pit in the ground the size you want your fire to be and about 10 inches (25 cm) deep. Surround the edge of the pit with large rocks.

STEP 5:

Place the tinder, such as small twigs, dry leaves, grass, and moss, in the bottom of the fire pit.

STEP 6:

Collect a selection of larger twigs, branches, and logs as fuel for your fire.

STEP 7:

To light the fire, fold a piece of newspaper in half three or four times.

STEP 8:

Take the bottle of water and use the rounded end of the bottle to catch the Sun's light and focus it onto the paper, like a magnifying glass. Aim for an area of paper where there is black ink because this will absorb more light.

Within a few seconds, the paper should begin smoldering and a small, smoldering hole will appear.

STEP 9:

Once the hole is about the size of a quarter, tuck the newspaper inside one of the folded sheets of paper. When that sheet begins to smolder, too, tuck the smoldering papers inside a second and then a third sheet of folded paper.

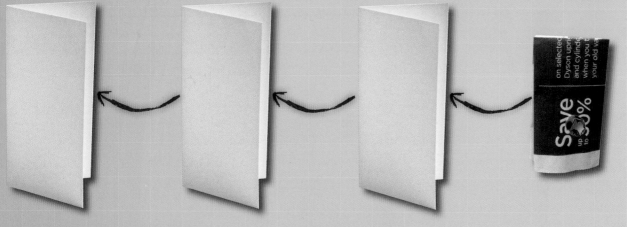

STEP 10:

Finally, gently waft the smoldering bunch of papers from side to side. A flame will appear and as the papers start to burn, carefully drop them into the fire pit on top of your dry tinder.

WARNING:

Only build and light a fire if an adult is there to help you.

FIRE SAFETY RULES

Always follow these rules when you make a fire.

- Store the wood for your fire upwind and away from the fire, so the wind isn't blowing the smoke toward the wood.
- Never leave a campfire unattended. An adult must stay with the fire at all times.
- Keep a bucket of water near the fire.
- Do not pull sticks or branches out of the fire.
- Always put out a fire by completely soaking it with water. Then stir the remains of the fire and completely soak with water again.
- Make sure the remains of the fire are cold before you leave the fire.

STEP 11:

When the small twigs and other dry materials are burning well, add larger twigs and finally branches and logs.

BUILD A SOLAR-POWERED OVEN

If you're camping, or simply spending time outdoors in your backyard, you might want to cook a snack.

If it's a hot, sunny day, there's no need to build a fire or go inside to use the microwave. You can use the Sun's power to heat food in a homemade oven.

A **solar-powered** oven can be made from an old file box, aluminum foil, and plastic wrap. The oven can be used to heat soup, beans, or other canned foods. You can even use it to make that all-time camping favorite, s'mores!

YOU WILL NEED:

• A file box
• A craft knife
• Aluminum foil
• Duct tape
• Sheet of black paper
• Plastic wrap
• A wire coat hanger
• A wire cutter

STEP 1:

Ask an adult to help you remove the spring-loaded clip from inside the file box.

STEP 2:

Cut a flap in the lid of the box.

Flap

File box

STEP 3:

Cover the inside of the box with aluminum foil and tape in place.

WARNING:

Only use a craft knife and wire cutters if an adult is there to help you.

STEP 4:
Place the sheet of black paper inside the box.

Closed lid of box

Foil-covered flap

STEP 5:
Close the lid of the box, leaving the flap outside. Cover the inside of the flap with foil and tape in place.

Black paper inside box

Plastic wrap stretched over hole

STEP 6:
Stretch plastic wrap over the hole in the box's lid and tape in place.

STEP 7:

To cook food in the oven, place the oven in a sunny spot. Open the lid and place the food on the black paper. Then close the lid so the plastic wrap is above the food.

STEP 8:

Cut a length of stiff wire from a coat hanger. Tape one end of the wire to the flap. Then position the flap at an angle so that the Sun shines onto the foil-covered flap and is reflected into the box. Once the flap is in the best position for capturing sunlight, tape the other end of the wire prop to the box to hold it in place.

STEP 9:

Here's how the solar-powered oven works. The Sun's light is reflected into the oven, creating heat. Inside the oven, the black paper absorbs the heat. The plastic wrap keeps the heat trapped inside the oven.

Sun reflecting off flap

Wire coat hanger prop

Food inside box beneath plastic wrap

LET'S GET SOLAR COOKING!

This fun project shows you how to make an outdoor cooler for food and drinks. The pot-in-a-pot cooler needs no electricity but uses **evaporation** of water to create a cooling effect. If you want your own **environmentally friendly** refrigerator in your backyard or at your campsite, try this project.

YOU WILL NEED:

- 2 unglazed terracotta flowerpots, sized so one fits inside the other leaving a gap
- Duct tape
- Sand
- Water
- A terracotta saucer or other shallow dish that covers the top of the smaller pot
- Dish towels

STEP 1:
Seal up the holes in the bottoms of the flowerpots with duct tape.

STEP 2:
Place enough sand in the bottom of the larger pot so that when the small pot is placed inside, the rims of the two pots are level.

STEP 3:
Fill the gap between the two pots with sand.

STEP 4:
Place your food and drink inside the cooler.

STEP 5:
Carefully pour water onto the sand. The sand will soak up the water, so keep pouring until all the sand is soaked, but don't allow it to get sloppy.

STEP 6:
Place the saucer on top as a lid, and fill the saucer with water.

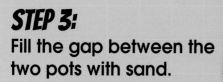

STEP 7:
Finally, cover the pots with wet dish towels.

The pot-in-a-pot cooler works because the heat outside of the pots will cause the water in the sand to evaporate. As water evaporates, it causes cooling. The temperature inside the pots will be many degrees cooler than outside!

STEP 8:
Add water to the sand when it dries out. For maximum cooling, keep refilling the saucer and wetting the dish towels, too.

anticipate (an-TIH-suh-payt)
To think about something in advance and plan for it.

compass (KUM-pus)
A device that shows you which direction you are traveling in. A compass has a needle that always points north, no matter which direction you are facing.

debris (duh-BREE)
The remains of something, or broken pieces of something. In a forest, debris might include fallen leaves and broken twigs and branches.

environmentally friendly
(in-vy-run-MEN-tul-ee FREND-lee)
Not damaging to the air, land, rivers, lakes, and oceans, or to plants and animals.

evaporation (ih-va-puh-RAY-shun)
The process by which liquid water becomes water vapor in the air. Water evaporates when it gets warm.

moss (MOS)
Low-growing plants that often cover rocks or trees and usually grow in damp places.

solar-powered (SOH-lur POW-urd)
Powered by energy from the Sun.

survival kit (sur-VY-vul KIT)
A collection of items that will be useful in an emergency situation or if a person is camping or living rough with few modern comforts. A kit might contain tools, medical equipment, and items used for cooking food.

utilize (YOO-tih-lyz)
To make use of.

wilderness (WIL-dur-nis)
A wild place where no humans live, such as a desert, forest, or on the slopes of a mountain.

wildfires (WYLD-fyrs)
Fires in natural habitats such as forests that are sometimes started by lightning, but are often started accidentally by people being careless when building campfires.

WEBSITES
Due to the changing nature of Internet links, Powerkids Press has developed an online list of websites related to the subject of this book. This site is updated regularly. Please use this link to access the list: www.powerkidslinks.com/dfb/rough/

READ MORE

Doeden, Matt. *Can You Survive the Wilderness?: An Interactive Survival Guide*. You Choose: Survival. Mankato, MN: Capstone Press, 2013.

Hardyman, Robyn. *Camping*. Adventures in the Great Outdoors. New York: Windmill Books, 2013.

Spilsbury, Louise. *How to Survive on a Mountain*. Tough Guides. New York: PowerKids Press, 2012.

INDEX

C
camp fires, 18–19, 20–21, 22–23
camping, 4, 24
compasses, 12–13
cooking, 4, 10, 24

D
debris huts, 14–15, 16–17

F
fire, 4, 10, 18–19, 20–21, 22–23
fishing equipment, 10

H
hiking, 4, 12

K
knives, 7, 8, 14

M
matches, 8, 18

P
projects to make:
build a forest shelter, 14–15, 16–17
build a solar-powered oven, 24–25, 26–27
building a campfire, 18–19, 20–21, 22–23
a DIY compass, 12–13
make a pot-in-a-pot cooler, 28–29

pocket-sized survival kit, 6–7, 8–9, 10–11

S
shelters, 4, 14–15, 16–17
solar-powered ovens, 4, 24–25, 26–27
survival kits, 4–5, 6–7, 8–9, 10–11, 12, 15

T
tents, 14

W
wild fires, 18
wilderness, 6, 12, 14